"YOU ENTER THE FOREST
AT THE DARKEST POINT
WHERE THERE IS NO PATH.

WHERE THERE IS A WAY OR PATH
IT IS SOMEONE ELSE'S PATH

YOU ARE NOT ON YOUR OWN PATH

IF YOU FOLLOW SOMEONE ELSE'S WAY
YOU ARE NOT GOING TO REALIZE
YOUR POTENTIAL"

-JOSEPH CAMPBELL ON THE HOLY GRAIL

Dedication:
With one eye on this world, one eye on the next, a third focused on the timeless. Through this life and all possible lifetimes, until universal enlightenment is achieved. May I, with the grace of the Divine, work tirelessly in awakening. Follow the path of unconditional compassion and selflessness, defeating illusion, to liberate myself, and all.

-July 2010

"I no longer try to change outer things. They are simply a reflection. I change my inner perception and the outer reveals the beauty so long obscured by my own attitude. I concentrate on my inner vision and find my outer vision transformed. I find myself attuned to the grandeur of life and in unison with the perfect order of the universe."
-The word. Book of runes by Ralph H. Blum
Also inscribed on the wall of the meditation room at Jolicoeur

Wake up Alice.

Wake up.

5

Wake up.

If I Go Living as Alice Dreams…

<u>WILL</u>

I am not a body
I am not a mind, nor am I words
I am my will

Bright and flickering
I blink out of this world
And into the next

Here, there is only silence
A silence that renders my physical self moot;
A self that knows only needs
Wrought with hungers that know no satisfaction
A self that is limited to know
Only what it sees.

TRAP

I am a trap
Of soft pink petals
Brown sugar
And sex.

We watch each other
Each pretending we are not.

You remind me of my humanness,
My flaws.
The hot animal wanting
For all the illusion
You lay before me.

I am a trap
My mind grasps at old
Beliefs about safety and survival
And binds me to the behaviours
That prove them

THE EMPTY TEMPLE

My body is a temple
To a skeletal God;
Of stillness and weakness,
Indulgence and rot.

Empty halls full of whispers
Of vain little ghosts
Who are trapped inside mirrors
But their image forgot.

HUNGER

Pity,
She had once been so pretty.
Until the hunger crawled
Out from the look in her eyes
And came to rest upon her lips,
Where it hangs silently,
Pretending to itself it isn't there.

It became her sentinel.
Her guardian against that which may
Destroy her,
Sustain her.

Pressed hard against her lips
Like a lover
Jealous,
Letting nothing else in.

VISION 1

It begins like this;
You are drawn up
And back
As if on the wings of a hawk
Hanging in an updraft.

From this vantage point
You can see the whole tapestry
Of your personal history
Animated by the wind of thought:
Kicking and bucking
So as the light of perception hits it
It throws up shadows
Which only seem
To be moving independently of their source.
Seem a whole drama unto themselves.

And suddenly
The wind stills.
The mind stops.
You are aware of the impossibly
Interconnected thing you had mistaken
For yourself.

It hums.

Something you interpret as sound
But is known without your ears.
It comes from within.

Trees creak and groan
Against one another
in their own secret language.

"I've never heard that before"
You say,
But you have,
You simply hadn't noticed it.

HALF MOON

Half moon
And the blood comes early.

Her sideways smile in the sky
Makes me wonder
What it is to be
Equal parts
Open and concealed.

PERU

My body:
"Are you coming back here?
Are you finally ready to rest in a moment?
No more franticly racing ahead,
No more returning to dwell
On that which you cannot change
That which no longer exists
(Maybe never has existed)

Are you ready to feel me?
I am full of hungers, and aches.
Long has the flesh been denied feeling,
for it knows no fulfillment.
To live in me is to ride the tides of fullness and
emptiness
And to find comfort
In the flux,
In the lull of sensation
The rising and falling waves
of pleasure and pain
Admitting that there is no final contentment
No total satisfaction, until death
And to not fear this fact.
I am your only real gift
On loan, from the earth, where I rose up from
And to which I will inevitably
Sink back into."

THE ONLY KEPT PROMISE

Breaking is the one
Promise our bodies really
Ever keep for us.

HABIT

A moody creature
Of habits
Only broken
The way you do
Fine china.

Simply drop it
In a thoughtless
Moment.

RESTLESSNESS

They whisper;
Stay.

But you won't.
Not because you can't
But because there are too many
Illusory doorways
Still unopened
Down the hallways of tomorrow.

Because once your knees
Had grown roots
Where you had knelt
At the feet
Of something that
Felt so much bigger
Than yourself.

And now without those roots
You need a current to feed you,
Like water passing over the gills
Of a salmon
Moving upstream
Returning to its origins.

THE MOJAVE DESERT

Road dogs, back on the black top.
Whipping through Sierra country-
The country of our first love.

Tall white armed giants wave
In cartwheels
Beckoning to a sustainable future
For these parched rust and terra-cotta coloured
hills.

Signs demand:
"Someone! Fix the water crisis"
Or "Chose life!"
And inevitably
"Jesus is Lord"

Everywhere people fly cardboard signs for the
Holidays.
California is stricken by drought
But it rains every God damn day
We are here.

THESE DAYS

I have been reconciling mirrors
And gathering strength.

I feel like a seed which has been firmly planted,
Finally,
After what felt like an eternity adrift
On a delicate white umbrella.

My roots mourn the memory
Of that breathless, unbound flight
Of the freedom and the comfort
In the knowledge that I could be carried
By the hand of the great unseen force
That it the wind.

I am like a creature newly emerged
From the cool wet pool of my childhood.
My new lungs burn with their first breaths.
My eyes and senses are a riot
Of fresh and overwhelming stimuli.

I am a woman mourning
The loss of the girl
Who dreamed me this life.

Dreams of serpents
Who's shiny black scales
Spoke to me of night
And void, the spaces between stars.

Who's bodies tell of streams
Which always move towards union
With the sea.

Dreams of panthers
Who wisely hide their splendour
And waste no time
Questioning their own ferocity.

I am a woman
Standing on the banks of
A great river
Gasping for breath
Wondering how I came ashore.

WOMANHOOD

As the rushing river
Draws nearer the sea
It calms, widens
And invites a certain slowness.

Full of promise
And anticipation
She is most powerful
in all the places
She draws and gathers to herself,
Each tributary an experience
Another path carved in her creation.

WANTON

As a woman
You're supposed to be pretty,
But not know
That you are.

And sex will be the first thing
Most men think about
When meeting you-

But you should hide
That you do the same.

SANTOSHA

Suffering happens
In the gap that exists
Between what you expected
And what is.

When you struggle
Fighting to close that space
You are in pain.

When you leap into that void
Accepting that it is there
You find yourself floating.
Suspended; held.
Touching neither side
Totally still.

DREAM

Alice sleeps
In a ray of sunshine
Dreaming worlds
She feels lost in.

The wind-chimes outside her bedroom window
Are the sounds
Of hundreds of tiny glass hearts
Shattering in the wake
Of her realization
That all she ever needed
Was herself.

ADDICT

Lately I've been uttering
Desperate prayers for the damned.
Those who walked to the edge,
That razor thin edge
Between creativity and destruction
And never walked backed.

But maybe,
They've escaped,
And it is us who need intercession.
For they've retreated back behind
The glass of their eyes
Back into the wild
Away from their broken, needy, bodies.

And as I stand
Pressing myself closer, trying to catch
One last glimpse,
It occurs to me that
Maybe we are the ones left in this zoo
Safe from the wilderness, but still captive.
And the screaming bodies
Left vacant by the souls that have abandoned
them;
In their chasing smoke and crystal,
And liquid forgetting,
Are our burdens to bear
For the many ways this cage we've built
Has failed them.

VAMPIRES AND THIEVES

There is this thing I do when I'm scared
I run into the arms
Of vampires and thieves.

Like a net
I let them wrap me up.
And the slaughter house feels like a temple
As they tear at my flesh
I go numb
And limp.
Safe; in the jaws of the beast.

LOSS

Loss you strange angel
Masquerading as death
What is it you are
Clearing the way for in my life?

Does it have to hurt so badly?

Will you hold my face
With one hand?
Whilst the other wields the knife
That is severing bonds
That were holding me in place.

VISIONS 2

Something opens.
Maybe eyes,
Maybe lips.

And there is a rushing
To fill
What is inherently empty.

Like a soft inhale
There is no real effort.
Only the breath moving in
Where space is made
By the void created
In relaxing
And letting go.

<u>CLEAN</u>

I crawled out of the skin
Of my old life
And into the warm tub
Of something new-
Let myself soak in it
Breathe in it's fumes.
My old life lay discarded on the floor
In a heap, stained and rumpled.
And I realized
I'll never dawn
Those clothes again.

RE-WILDING

Was it all a betrayal of her power?
That she could have what she asked for
At the price of;
The loss of his sanity,
Their love.
Her struggle to be free.

Freedom;
That mythic Goddess she did worship-
Cruel God, as often as not.

It's worth noting many animals
Kept captive too long
Die when you return them
To the wild.

ALTER

Sometimes reckoning is like a remembering.
Sometimes you are blessed to forget.

Given just a tiny token maybe;
A fragile seashell,
A feather dusty pink,
A shark's tooth shaped like a can opener-
Meant to peel away a turtles shell.

These things take on different meanings
As we retell the story to ourselves.
Do the objects themselves hold latent power?
Or are they merely titles,
Book marks maybe,
Making us recall moments
of the story to which they belong.
What if we chose novel ways
To tell ourselves these stories?

INITIATION

I will not seek to see
Or understand
But I will sit with open hands
Simultaneously offering up
And awaiting to receive
The hand of God
Who will lead me
Down the path
Only I may walk.

MIRROR MIRROR

Sometimes reflections lie,
The light plays tricks and your eyes
Flicker over some imagined masses
Where really only space exists.

You are seeing how you feel
About yourself;
Too much, too big, too loud.
Messy and soft,
Frayed edges and
Ultimately,
A tempest.

You blink and remind yourself
That these perceptions are mirages.
You've been in this hall of mirrors before.
You're feeling around in the dark for that exit
But keep bumped up against
Your own image.

Foolish, selfish girl
You are a strange maze,
Aren't you?

Pressing your body against the glass
As if it were something warm
That might love you back,
You whisper to yourself on repeat
Ad nauseam,

"its not real."

But the feelings ARE real.
They rise like a tide
Over the storm walls
To threaten the home you've built there.
They poison the ground water,
But you can't help but
Return to drink from that well.

OF HAVING AND LOSS

The world holds a paradox
In it's crushing perfection and beauty,
And it's capacity to suffer and cause suffering.

Having and loss
Stand hand in hand as teachers.
Both are attachment,
And are as human
As war.

Having is our Mother,
Bringing us into the world;
With connection and touch,
Warm comfort and security.

Loss is our Father,
Who births in us longing, feeling,
Challenges us
Through him we learn art.

We are complete
When we stand apart from them both.

Suspended in the aether
Bodies dissolved and free from
The tyranny of form,
The demands of
Hungers and passions.

Empty of tears,
Hands open,
Not waiting to receive
Or grasping what has left
But as a gesture of openness itself
Ready to take up
The real work
Our hands were made to do.

RED WOLF

We would sit on the street corner,
And sneer at the beautiful people of the city
Drinking whiskey and smoking
Howling with defiance
With out stretched hands,
Ignorant in our innocence
To the irony
Of surviving on the overflow from purses
We cursed with our words.

We fancied ourselves wise in those days.
Days we spent chasing Virgin Marys
With our torn stockings,
cigarettes hanging from our lips.
We'd declare our love for one another,
Over and over in frenzies
And strut with the confidence of
Those who had not yet tasted real loss.

With saucer eyes
We'd lay traps for lesser mortals,
And our prey would provide for us
As any pack would.
We were tribal and wild.
And this illusion of freedom
Poisoned us against
Caring for our soft, fragile bodies
Which we vehemently battled against.

We courted damnation like a lover
And laughed
When it came bearing gifts
Mistaking our interest
For commitment.

Because we, we eternal.
Always above.

You were my Dragon,
A force of fiery wrath
And breathless beauty
Myths were written in your wake.

And I was the shapeshifter,
Everything and nothing-
But yours.

And who could resist you?

So I wept freely
As though the water might extinguish
The flames that grew around you
As I watched you burn at the stake
You'd tied yourself to.
All the while spitting accusations
Curses against the witch hunt
Only you were living.

Calling for help
Then biting the hands
That tried to free you.

How like you,
Red Wolf,
To gnash your teeth and snarl.
You have always been wild.
And at least if this is how you go
You go true to your nature.

AMONGST WILD FLOWERS

Riots of blooms
On an overgrown road,
Reclaimed in tangles
Of soft petals and thorns.

I count myself among them
In this undomesticated eden
In disturbed, upturned earth.
Thriving in a scar upon the land
A garden given chance to grow,
Not in spite of
But because of the destruction
Once wrought here.

STOLEN

Poems are often stolen
From the edges of my mind
Before they can be born of my hands
Or my tongue
By this little glass screen.
Like an obsidian mirror;
An abyss of opportunities
To compare myself to this
Angel or that Goddess,
With an impossible body
And glistening hair.

Into that looking glass
I continue to stare
And pin up
My own un-doctored images
My resolution
To love my body,
As it is.

UPSWELL

I feel that upwelling
Myself lifted upon the crest
Of a great wave.
One I know will eventually break
And toss me,
Laughing and spent
Back onto the sand
Dishevelled and battered
By the ride.
I've come to know
How to read the tides
And how to savour
These moments
These highs.
Because before long
The swell is gone,
And in it's place
The beach is pockmarked
In tiny wretched pools.
Each a universe unto itself-
Revealing that which the waves
So carefully concealed.
A place to trace barefoot trails
And over turn stones.
A place where the evidence of your searching
Will be annihilated
By the next exalting swell.

COVEN

Smoke rises in serpentine tendrils
Reminding me of my great teacher
Who showed me how to shed my skin
To shrug off the grief
Of the life I'd outgrown.

She showed me how to move;
To charm with waves
Rippling my form
Drawing her energy skyward
Kundalini rising
Dancing; with just my heart
Keeping time.

The music is always within me
And in trance
Her song is pulled from my lips
Shyly at first,
But she is calling it from me
Who am I to deny her?

So I sing:
Prayers for my sisters,
That in them she awakens
So that in turn
Each may see herself
Reflected in herSelf.

This connection
Shared between us,
Echoed in ourselves,
Like chords of white light
That becomes a path.

Moonlight,
Salt,
And moonblood.

In the silence that followed
I was bathed and made pure
And blank,
As blank as the page revealed
As the the moon turned
To it's next phase.

NEW MOON

The tide comes up
Swallows the shore line
And I begin to wade out to sea
Which stretches out before me in all directions.
It is both;
The place where I once crawled out from
And the place to which I am returning.

The mother's hands caress my body
In tiny, lapping waves
Until my feet can barely touch.

I am standing at the threshold
Here there is no place to build my alter
Save inside myself.
No place to kneel
So each step I take deeper
Is my prayer.

AUTUMN

The veil grows thinner
And the mind opens
Like some dark flower.
In the stillness
And the darkness behind your eyes
This night bloom unfolds
Offering sweetness at it's very centre.
You are ever drawn towards it
By its seductive perfume.

THE PLACE NO MAN TOUCHES

Keep apart of yourself
For yourself
As you pass out the bread
Of your body
Like mass;
To feed the masses.

And though it might be true
It is you who hath sustained him
Who is feeding you?
Tenderly from the palm of his hand
Because lest you find yourself
Eating from the palm
Of some man's hand
And completely at his whim.

Keep a part of yourself
For yourself
And keep it wild!
Let the grass grow there
In thick tangles, dotted with weeds
And wild flowers.
So as to give a home
To all your secret thoughts
And watch as these private musings
Plant seeds and grow to bear fruit
That is yours and yours alone to relish.

And when you come back to the world,
Fingers sticky and mouth satined,
From the sweet juices
Of your mind
They will press themselves to you;
Kissing at the corners of your mouth
And sucking at your fingers,
Just to try to taste
What you have hidden.

ORIGINS 1

I pull a dress over my head
And wriggle into it.
It's freshly washed
For the first time in months.
The smell of the detergent
And the vaguely moldy smell,
Layered together
Like icing on a cake
Reminds me of my father,
And my throat tightens slightly.

Diesel, wood-shops, fresh paint
Old, un-rinsed beer cans left out
In the sun
Un-washed laundry
Each of these smells can catch me unaware,
Some passing memory grips me
And these moments
Drift up
From a time
When he was my hero.

Back before trouble
Could be seen
Through the veil of my innocence.

ORIGINS 2

When the sun came up
I went out to the deck
To take up the seat
Where the evening before
I had found her
Quietly wiping tears from her eyes.

I sat and looked out onto the yard
Trying to pull from the air
her lingering presence here
As if maybe the heat of her body
Had made a mark upon the spot
And impression I could feel,
If only I was still enough,
That might offer some secret bridge
To cross that profound disconnect
Between what she says to me with words
And what her eyes are telling me.

Eyes like looking in a mirror
But on the other side of the glass
Is a woman of such mystery-
Is my origins.
How can I come to know myself?
When before me is this flesh and blood woman
From which my flesh was made
And of who sometimes
I feel like I know nothing.

I can feel her, protective
Holding back and seeing
My mistakes as her mistakes.

But what else can we do
The women like us
Who's hearts have been broken
Who've known betrayal and loss
But turn our bodies into weapons
Our smiles into shields.
Mine these days tastes bitter
Bitter as the black coffee
I drink by her example.

It happened
The tears came- and I felt
The pain
That is born in the gap
That lives between us,
In the distortion that twists
Our words when we speak
As if all our conversations are under water.

OPEN SKY

Sky
I am
Arms open
Face turned towards heaven
Turned inward
I am
Sky.

FAMILY SHADOW

You walked through the fires of your initiation
And spent the first turns
Of your adult life
Tending those wounds.
You were marked early
Not chosen
But swallowed by circumstance,
The yawning maw
Of your family shadow
Leaving impressions on your mind
Like bruises on a body.

But nothing is broken
The places where the mirror
Has been cracked
So as to scatter your reflection
Into tiny fractured portraits
Are the places through
Which you can squeeze,
Escaping this illusion
Created by an unmoving
Crystal surface
That would give you the impression
Of a single image
Who's depth cannot be probed
As you press your finger
To it's cool, smooth
Unfeeling surface.

Bring your body to these edges
And you may cut yourself open upon them,
Again revealing the hidden nature
Of what is contained within.

As you pass through the cracks
In the mirror
Held before you; like a veil
A Vision is Gifted.
You're shaking,
But you're free.

TORINO

A palace resplendent in Baroque
Speckled in gold,
A city to hold
A stained veil
Drenched in blood
Fabled; the blood of a messiah.

A market crawls
With the young and
Those not from here.

Riots;
Of colour, smell
Rebellion;
When the police
Place walls to block stalls,
Block the mouth of immigrant children and
The self organizing
Organism
That is the soul of the city.

Tables full of food
Offerings to old Gods
Of friendship, hearth
And hospitality
Welcome arms and warmth.

They will crawl back into
Abandoned buildings

And stoke the fire
From the inside
To keep
That soul alive.

HRIDAYA

November skies
Open above the hamlet
Hinting at an expanse
Of powder blue
Only temporarily obscured
By the moody season
Who's frequent tempests swell
The springs
And tear the last clinging,
Grasping leaves
From branches,
Who's gentle teaching
Is simply;
Let go.

After what seems like endless rain
The True Sky;
That still, clear backdrop
Upon which the weather
Opens and closes it's curtains;
Playing out dramas and comedies
Opens up and stretches out,
Like silence.

TAPAS

Dedication is the way
The soft discipline
Of the path of devotion

DAYDREAMS OF WEST COAST WATERS IN AMSTERDAM

I feel I am
Like the soft pink body
Of an anemone
Reaching out of need
Into the open arms of the sea
To let herself be fed
By the currents,
Lest there be
Some minor disturbance
And she puckers, self protective
Retreats.

Into that tight coil
Where she knows no fear
But no nourishment,
Can be neither fed or admired,
Neither destroyed or desired.

HECATE

Words come like visitations
Drifting up to me
Like smoke
From the hot ember
Deep in my core.

Twisting tendrils
Of hidden meaning
All whispering
Of snakes.

FORGIVING MYSELF FIRST

I've waged war
With myself
Without humility
Like a tyrant.
I've starved and shamed
Myself
Because I am
Imperfect.

Rage;
Against these beliefs
Laid out before you,
Careful traps
To keep you struggling
Near the surface
Away from the depth
Of power
That lives
Down a street you walk at night,
That you've been warned
All your life,
Is too dangerous for you to take.

It can only be felt
When you are alone
And so they give you
A guard, a chaperone,
To protect you
From hungry eyes

That both urge you to undress
And damn
And rape you
When you do.

Rage;
Against myself
For buying in
And turning
A pretty painted face
Towards the masses
Begging to be loved
As only a beautiful woman
Can be loved.

Rage;
For energies spent
Not on studies
Or skills
Or even kindness
But on
Carefully rewiring my brain
To feel ecstasy when starving.
To crave nothing
That might give me strength enough
To rebel.

I've waged war
With myself
When I could have been
My ally
And joined myself to myself

Struggled free of
The lovely gilded cage
To risk
The danger
Of undomestication .

A woman unkept
Finally free.

DESIRE

Consumptive
Is the fire;
Desire burns bright
Turning that which is fed to it
Into inertia that
Spins the wheel
The engine
That guides the hand
Back to the mouth,
Not to nourish,
But to dig deeper the well.
Creating the illusion of need
Which sees men
Drinking from the sea
To meet their thirst
Despite the ever present
Rain.

FELINE LESSONS

Stretch and observe
Move with grace
Keep my range wide
And my own counsel.

For a cat may look upon a king
And a tiger,
Striking and regal,
Need not stand out in the open
To be counted
As lord of her domain.

A PATH BETWEEN PATHS

Bells ring
From the tower
But I do not fear change
For I have walked
The brimstone landscapes
Of past actions
And across barren sands
To be cooled by the ocean;
The beginning.

I've been entranced by it's edge
Where the horizon
Melts sky and sea together.
I've chased that line
Watching the sun vanish behind it
And be born again
In the mountains at my back.
I've learned that to be
Free of that circle,
The only way it up- as if
To break the crust of the atmosphere
And let myself be spread thin
As the sky.

But my place is here
On the path between paths
Each step a prayer,
A celebration,
Not a hurried expedition

Because I have no destination,
The path itself
Is home.

THE WIND

I knew you not
Though you were all around me
An unseen voice
Offering to lift me up.
I felt your presence
When you would carry tendrils of smoke
From the incense on my alter
To wash my mind
Of the day to day
And orientate me to Spirit,
Of which you are
Her breath.

SUMMER

Black berry,
Lilac,
And wisteria.
Back lit foliage at dawn
Golden light seeping
Through my sheer dress
To run a pale finger
Across my skin.

PAST AND PRESENT

The Mediterranean sun
Teases memories
From just below the surface
As I weave around the coast
I'm joined
By my innocent ghost
Who a decade ago
Tread pathways through
Andean dust
And felt just as free.

I can re-claim her bravery
And forgive her foolishness
As I recall words spoken to me
By a dreamer
Just past the crest of the equinox
When I was born to the path
That I am awakening upon.

I blink,
And as my eyes open
They are filled with the azure
Of the sea.
I walk until the cliffs
Crumble into soft sand,
Where I lay and watch
The hills swallow the sun.

Like a great animal
Upon the open plains,
I was born
On the move
Pulled by the invisible
Force of migration.
That seasonal river
Of life seeking more life
Satiating its thirst
As it escapes the droughts
And claims new verdant lands
Heavy with promise
Of renewal.

TEMPLE

My only protection is right action.
I lay an offering on the alter
Of the temple of my body
And in the stillness
What is offered creates waves
Like tiny ripples on a pond
Expanding over the velvet dark
Gentle waves that build
Into forces such as storms
That break against unseen shores
Creating and destroying.
The vibratory shapes of causality
Who's winds are born
In a soft, and thoughtful breath.
Who's bodies of water
Are the fabric of existence itself
A woven tapestry of which this prayer
Is but a single thread.

FOR KARINA

The pen can be a mirror
By giving birth
To what was once subtle,
Unto the substantial.
Crossing the gossamer threshold
Between the manifest and un-manifest realms.
Casting spells
By spelling out
Using mundane symbols
These characters become a tool
For reflection.
Allowing us to glimpse
The imperceivable.
Making solid
That which is ever shifting.
Making tangible a moment
Of the Ephemeral,
Eternal, internal
Worlds of
Spirit and mind.

FIN

Focus on the exhale
As you empty yourself of
What is no longer serving-
You make space
For the breath
That will sustain you.

Soften and opens your hands,
And life will rush
To fill them.

Resist the temptation
To close again your fingers,
Hungrily clutching
That which is offered anew,
For in another moment
It too passes into autumn,
Becomes dry and brittle,
And you will be left
Squeezing a fist full of sand.

Weep not as it runs
Between your fingers,
But revel in the sensation,
Like silk over your delicate skin,
Kissing you good-bye-
As it falls at your feet
To become the verdant path of spring
Which beckons you ever forward

And from where
The seeds of your heart
Can be planted,
Fed by the death
Of all of your past moments
To create the garden of your life
All around you.

Hands closed around
Any gift
Are not free
To till the soil
And pick the fruits
Of your labours.

Hands open
Move quickly
When called
Touching each task fully
But lightly.

So focus on the exhale
And offer, palms turned upward
What is in your hands
To the earth at your feet
To feed her.

And trust
In your inherent ability
To feed yourself
From the engagement of this cycle
To which you have been initiated.

Call yourself Priestess
Empty and ripe.
Full like the moon
A reflection of light.
Pregnant with your own potential
Birthed in letting go
Of any idea of mastery.

Wild in the garden
An untamed thing.
Containing the paradox
Of cultivating oneself
And allowing what is
To simply be.

END.

ABOUT THE AUTHOR

Felicia Davis-Gosling, otherwise known as Fish, or Goldie Glitteris, is a Canadian tree planter, yoga teacher and hypnotherapist who spends most of her time on Vancouver Island. Her single goal and desire for life is to continue to cultivate a more honest and intimate relationship to herSelf, in hopes to be of service to others in healing their own relationships to Self.